ASIA

ALICIA KLEPEIS

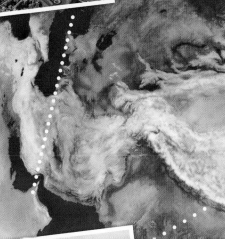

Rourke
Educational Media
rourkeeducationalmedia.com

Before & After Reading Activities

Before Reading:

Building Academic Vocabulary and Background Knowledge

Before reading a book, it is important to tap into what your child or students already know about the topic. This will help them develop their vocabulary, increase their reading comprehension, and make connections across the curriculum.

1. *Look at the cover of the book. What will this book be about?*
2. *What do you already know about the topic?*
3. *Let's study the Table of Contents. What will you learn about in the book's chapters?*
4. *What would you like to learn about this topic? Do you think you might learn about it from this book? Why or why not?*
5. *Use a reading journal to write about your knowledge of this topic. Record what you already know about the topic and what you hope to learn about the topic.*
6. *Read the book.*
7. *In your reading journal, record what you learned about the topic and your response to the book.*
8. *After reading the book complete the activities below.*

Content Area Vocabulary

Read the list. What do these words mean?

continents
ethnic groups
Fertile Crescent
gamelan
hemispheres
lichens
monarchies
monsoon
service jobs
species
steppes

After Reading:

Comprehension and Extension Activity

After reading the book, work on the following questions with your child or students in order to check their level of reading comprehension and content mastery.

1. What kinds of plants and animals live in Asia? (Summarize)
2. What differences might a visitor notice when traveling from one Asian country to another? (Infer)
3. What kinds of struggles or challenges have people in Asia faced throughout its history? (Asking Questions)
4. Which Asian landmarks would you most like to visit? Why? (Text to Self Connection)
5. What kinds of activities do people in Asia enjoy in their free time? (Asking Questions)

Extension Activity

After reading the book, try this activity. Pick an Asian country you are interested in and research its capital city. What kinds of places does this city offer for tourists to visit? What language(s) are spoken here? How does this city compare to where you live? Draw a simple map of the city, labeling any natural features (rivers, mountains, etc.).

Table of Contents

Countries in Asia:

- Afghanistan
- Armenia
- Azerbaijan
- Bahrain
- Bangladesh
- Bhutan
- Brunei
- Cambodia
- China
- Georgia
- India
- Indonesia
- Iran
- Iraq
- Israel
- Japan
- Jordan
- Kazakhstan
- Kuwait
- Kyrgyzstan
- Laos
- Lebanon
- Malaysia
- Maldives
- Mongolia
- Myanmar
- Nepal
- North Korea
- Oman
- Pakistan
- Philippines
- Qatar
- Russia
- Saudi Arabia
- Singapore
- South Korea
- Sri Lanka
- Syria
- Tajikistan
- Thailand
- Timor-Leste (East Timor)
- Turkey
- Turkmenistan
- United Arab Emirates
- Uzbekistan
- Vietnam
- Yemen

Welcome to Asia!

Raging rivers. Incredible islands. Massive mountains. Asia has all of these things—and much more.

Asia is the largest of the world's seven **continents**. It covers

Asia's Fast Facts
Population
• More than 4.5 billion people live in Asia.
• Asia is home to about 60 percent of the world's total population.
Land Size
• 17,212,000 square miles (44,579,000 square kilometers)
Other Data
• biggest urban area – Tokyo-Yokohama (37.8 million people)

more land and has more people than any other continent. Asia covers an area of 17.2 million square miles (44.6 million square kilometers). That's more than four times the size of the United States!

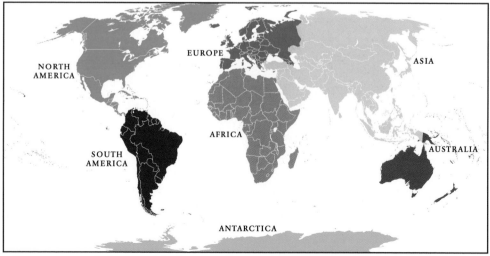

This image of the world shows all seven continents.

Where is Asia? Most of it is in the Northern and Eastern **hemispheres**. Several water bodies border Asia. North of Asia is the Arctic Ocean. To the east is the Pacific Ocean. South of Asia lies the Indian Ocean. The Ural Mountains form the western boundary of Asia. They divide Asia from Europe.

Asia has many landscapes. It has mountain systems. It has plains, deserts, and **steppes**. There are also saltwater and freshwater environments here.

This political map shows all of the countries in Asia.

Many mountain ranges are in Asia. The Kunlun and Altay (or Altai) Mountains are two examples. Some of the world's highest mountains are located in the Himalayas. People from around the world travel to climb these mountains.

Lots of rivers flow through Asia. The Yangtze, Tigris, and Euphrates are three major ones.

People who enjoy hiking in the mountains have many options in Asia.

India and Southeast Asia are affected greatly by **monsoon** season. Monsoons are seasonal changes in the direction of the winds in a region. They cause both dry and wet seasons in much of the tropics. From about April to September, the summer monsoon brings heavy rains. Farmers depend on these rains to grow their crops.

The sand dunes of the Arabian Desert are constantly shifting because of the winds here.

Asia has some huge desert areas. The Arabian Desert is located in southwestern Asia. Not many people live here. It's too hot and dry. The Gobi Desert is in China and Mongolia. This desert is hot in the summer and cold in the winter. It even snows here!

Animal and Plant Life

Many different plants and animals live in Asia. Some are not found anywhere else on Earth.

Because the climate of Asia is so varied, the plants that live here are too. Spruce and birch trees grow in northern Asia. So do **lichens** and mosses. Farther south are grasslands. Eastern Asia is home to bamboo forests where rare animals like the giant panda live. And beech and evergreen trees are found in the mountains of southwest Asia.

A walking path invites people to explore the Arashiyama Bamboo Forest in Kyoto, Japan.

Rainforests are common in South and Southeast Asia. Tropical flowers like orchids and Rafflesia grow here. Rafflesia flowers can be three feet (.91 meters) across. They smell like rotting meat to attract insects!

A young man discovers a Rafflesia flower while hiking.

Plants that live in Asia's deserts must be able to survive with little water. Sedges are plants that grow in sandy areas. They have deep roots.

Russia is home to a huge area of taiga or boreal forest. This forested area is found just south of the Arctic Circle. Coniferous trees like pine and spruce grow here. So do mosses and mushrooms. Siberian tigers make their home in the taiga. Moose, bears and lynx live here too.

Just like its plants, Asian animals are diverse. King cobras and Komodo dragons are two Asian reptiles. Some mammals are found only in Asia. The Indian rhinoceros and orangutan are two examples.

Orangutans spend about 90 percent of their time in the trees of the tropical rainforests where they live.

Yaks are animals related to buffalo and bison. They are very important to the people of Tibet. People use yaks to carry heavy loads in the mountains. The Tibetan people also get meat and milk from yaks. And the wool from these animals can be used to make very warm clothing.

Colorful birds are kept in cages waiting to be sold as pets in an Asian market.

Asia is home to thousands of bird **species**. Spice finches, birds of paradise, and the Bali myna are just a few. Sadly, some are caught illegally to be sold as pets.

History & Government

Three of the world's earliest civilizations were located in Asia. An area known as the **Fertile Crescent** is often described as "the birthplace of agriculture." Nomadic peoples made their homes along the riverbanks. About 10,000 years ago, they harvested wild barley and wheat here. They also raised animals such as pigs, sheep, and cows.

Over time, communities in the region grew. Since not everyone needed to farm, people could do other things. They developed trade, religion, and writing.

Once a sleepy fishing village, the city of Kaş is located on the Mediterranean Sea. Today it is popular with tourists.

The Indus River Valley was another important historical site. This early civilization developed around 2500 BCE. People here built durable structures from stone and brick. Cities had homes, temples, and warehouses. They also had walls to protect them from invaders.

Buddhism is an Asian religion which began in India and Nepal around the late 6th century BCE. Traders and other travelers spread this religion by both land and sea routes. Today Buddhism is the most popular religion in much of eastern Asia. More than 46% of the world's Buddhists live in China.

Structures of many shapes and sizes are built into the rocky terrain of this Indus River Valley site.

There have been many conflicts over religion for thousands of years in the area known as the Holy Land (located in Southwest Asia). In particular, these conflicts have been among Jews, Christians, and Muslims. Sadly, these conflicts continue even today.

The city of Jerusalem is home to many religious sites, such as the Church of the Holy Sepulchre (with its silver dome shown in front).

From the 1500s until the mid-20th century, many Southeast Asian peoples were ruled by colonial powers from Europe, Japan, and the U.S. Often these nations wanted to rule Asian lands to increase trade, get cheap raw materials, and make lots of money. Today the countries of Southeast Asia are independent.

Not all Asian countries have the same type of government. Several countries are **monarchies**. Examples include Bhutan and Jordan. The kings and queens do not always run the government. Other Asian nations like Singapore have a republican form of government. The people elect officials who represent their interests in the government.

King Jigme Khesar Namgyel Wangchuck of Bhutan

The People of Asia

About 4.5 billion people live in Asia. This is more than half of all the people on Earth. Asians belong to many different **ethnic groups**. These groups often have their own ways of life, celebrations, and traditions. For example, the Malay people live in Malaysia and parts of Southeast Asia. They speak a language called Malay. Historically parents have arranged marriages for their children. Traditional Malay houses are set off the ground. This protects people from flooding and wild animals.

This traditional Bugis house is on display at a museum in Selangor, Malaysia.

People in Asia speak more than 2,300 different languages. Arabic is the most commonly spoken language in Southwest Asia. Hindi is the most popular in India. More people in China speak Mandarin than any other language. Russian and English are also often used in Asia.

Arab schoolchildren enjoy many of the same activities as other kids around the world.

More than seven million people call Hong Kong home. People in this crowded city live in many kinds of housing. Many live in high-rise apartment buildings. The wealthiest people may have fancy, single-family homes. Some people choose to dwell on houseboats in the harbor. And the poorest residents live in cubicle-like spaces.

All of the world's major religions began in Asia. The main religion in India and Nepal is Hinduism. Many Southwest Asian people practice Islam. This religion is also popular in Indonesia, Pakistan, Bangladesh and Malaysia. Israel's main religion is Judaism. Some people practice Christianity throughout Asia. But it's only the main religion in Armenia, Russia, and the Philippines.

The Hindu festival of Holi involves throwing colorful powders into the air as a celebration of spring.

People in Asia do different types of work. In many Asian countries, agriculture is still a major part of the economy. Farmers grow rice, wheat, tea, sugarcane, and other crops. Fishing is also a common way to earn money in coastal nations.

Throughout Asia, many workers have **service jobs**. They work in schools, hospitals, shops, and museums. Asian factory workers produce all kinds of goods from computers to sneakers.

A traditional fisherman is at work on the Li River in China. The cormorants (birds) help him catch fish, thanks to snares tied around their throats (so they can't swallow big fish).

Food & Fun

Like people around the globe, Asians enjoy good food. They also like to have fun. People in Asia create terrific music, art, literature, and dance.

Throughout history, Asian musicians have written and performed a wide variety of music. Some songs use traditional instruments or tell folktales from a particular culture. **Gamelan** music comes from Indonesia. In this type of music, many instruments are played such as bronze gongs, drums, flutes, and stringed instruments. Singers sometimes accompany the music.

An Indonesian boy plays a percussion instrument called the bonang during a parade on the island of Bali.

K-pop is a popular kind of music. It began in South Korea but is loved around the world now. K-pop is a mixture of hip-hop, electronic, rock, and R&B music styles. Performers in this genre often have incredible dance moves. "Gangnam Style" is a popular K-pop song by the artist Psy.

SARY

ARDS

Activity.

Make A Hanging Koi (Fish)

Koi are a type of fish commonly found in Japan. They can come in a variety of bright colors. Many Japanese gardens have ponds where koi fish swim. Make your own hanging koi to decorate your room or home.

Supplies:

- Construction paper
- Colored scraps of paper (from old magazines, catalogs, junk mail, etc.)
- Aluminum foil
- Quarter or circular bottle top
- Scissors
- Crayons or markers
- Glue
- Stapler
- Hole punch
- Ribbons or crepe paper streamers
- Yarn or string

Directions:

1. Draw a koi fish on a piece of construction paper. You can look for a picture of these fish online or in a book.

2. Place another piece of construction paper under the first one. Cut through both pieces of paper. You will end up with two fish this way.

3. On the colorful scrap paper and aluminum foil, trace around the quarter or bottle top to make lots of circles. Cut these circles out using scissors.

4. Glue these circles onto both sides of the fish's body. (These are the two fish shapes you cut out.) Remember that you want the scales to be on the outside of the fish when you staple the two fish shapes together.

5. Use markers or crayons to decorate the fish's tail, fins, and head.

6. Staple the two sides of your fish together. Be sure the scales are on the outside. Staple your ribbons or crepe paper streamers inside the fish's tail.

7. Punch a hole into the fish's face. Put string or yarn from this hole. Hang up and enjoy!

People enjoy many sports in Asia. One of the most popular is cricket. This game is played with a bat and ball. Badminton is well-liked across Asia. So is table tennis.

Visitors from around the globe travel to Asia for vacation. Some islands are particularly popular. Bali, Indonesia is one example. Phuket in Thailand and Singapore are others. People enjoy the beautiful beaches and cultural sites of these islands.

A gibbon rests in a tree. Gibbons can move through the jungle as fast as 35 miles (56.3 kilometers) per hour.

Asia is home to many national parks. Phou Khao Khouay National Park is located in Laos. This huge park is home to gibbons, a type of ape. Wild elephants also live here. Beautiful orchids thrive in the wet season. Visitors can hike to see lakes, jungle, mountains, and waterfalls.

Food is an important part of Asian culture. Different nations often have their own special meals or desserts. But common ingredients or spices can be part of the food in particular regions. For example, people in Southwest Asia often eat lentils, chickpeas, and olive oil. Seafood is a big part of the diet for many Asians. Rice is also commonly eaten, especially throughout East and Southeast Asia.

Noodle dishes are popular in many parts of Asia. This woman is eating hers with chopsticks.

Recipe: Easy Asian Noodles

Noodle dishes are popular in many Asian countries.

Ingredients:

7 ounces (200 grams) dried noodles (can be rice or egg noodles)
2 scallions, thinly sliced
1 large carrot, grated
2 ounces (56 grams) (a small handful) green beans, thinly sliced
2 teaspoons (10 milliliters) vegetable/canola oil
1 garlic clove, finely chopped
3-4 ounces (84 to 113 grams) firm tofu, cut into small cubes (optional)
water
Sauce:
1 tablespoon (15 milliliters) soy sauce
2 teaspoons (10 milliliters) honey
1 teaspoon (5 milliliters) (tomato) ketchup
Juice of half a lemon

Directions:

1. Place the noodles in a heatproof bowl. Have an adult help to pour boiling water over the noodles until they are covered. Let the noodles sit (and cook) for about 5 minutes. Then drain the noodles and rinse them under cold water.

2. In a small bowl, mix the lemon juice, soy sauce, honey and ketchup.

3. Have an adult heat the oil in a pan on the stove. Add the garlic to the pan and stir for about 30 seconds.

4. Add green beans, carrots, and scallions to the pan. Then add the cubed tofu, if using. Stir-fry these ingredients for about 3-4 minutes. Add the sauce and one to two tablespoons (15-30 milliliters) of water.

5. Add the cooked noodles to the pan on the stove. Stir all the ingredients for a few minutes. Remove the pan from the stove. Enjoy the meal!

Landmarks

Some of the world's most amazing landmarks are located in Asia. Here are just a few of these beautiful buildings and spectacular sites!

The Burj Khalifa in Dubai is currently the world's tallest building. It stands 2,717 feet (828 meters) high. That's more than half a mile up in the air!

Petra is an ancient Arab city in Jordan. Its name is taken from the Greek word for "rock." Many of Petra's buildings were built right into the sandstone cliffs. People come from all over the world to visit Petra.

The Burj Khalifa dominates the skyline of Dubai. It cost $1.5 billion and took 12,000 workers to build.

Millions of tourists visit Angkor Wat each year. Angkor was the center of the Khmer Kingdom for several centuries.

Cambodia is home to a 12th century temple called Angkor Wat. It's the biggest religious structure on Earth. Angkor Wat's ruins stretch over 150 square miles (400 square kilometers). This temple was originally built to honor the Hindu god Vishnu. But it later was converted for use by Buddhist people.

The Forbidden City is located in Beijing, China. This complex of palaces and administrative buildings was built in the 15th century. Twenty-four Chinese emperors lived here. It was called Forbidden City because common people weren't allowed here. But today it's a museum for everyone to visit.

Glossary

continents (KANT-uhn-entz): the world's great divisions of land, such as Europe or North America

ethnic groups (ETH-nik GRUPZ): populations or communities of people who share a common cultural tradition or descent

Fertile Crescent (FURT-uhl KRES-unt): an area of rich, farmable land in the Middle East extending from the eastern coast of the Mediterranean to the Persian Gulf

gamelan (GAM-uh-lan): a traditional Indonesian grouping of instruments, often including lots of bronze percussion instruments

hemispheres (HEM-uh-sfeerz): the halves of the Earth, as divided by either the equator or the prime meridian

lichens (LEYE-kuhnz): slow-growing plants which normally form a crustlike or leaflike growth on rocks, trees, or walls

monarchies (MAHN-uhr-keez): countries or nations ruled by monarchs (especially kings, queens, or emperors)

monsoon (mahn-SOON): a seasonal change in the winds of a region, particularly in South and Southeast Asia

service jobs (SUHR-viss JOBZ): jobs in which a worker provides some type of useful labor but does not produce goods

species (SPEE-sheez): a category of living things, made up of related individuals that can produce offspring

steppes (STEPZ): large areas of unforested, flat grasslands found in Siberia and southeastern Europe

Index

Show What You Know

1. Where is Asia located?

2. What are some places in Asia where people go to vacation?

3. How does Asia compare in size to the other continents?

4. What is the weather in Asia like?

5. What kinds of jobs do people have in Asia?

Further Reading

Adventures Around the Globe, Lonely Planet Kids, 2015.

Williams, Rachel, Atlas of Adventures, Wide Eyed Editions, 2015.

Kalman, Bobby and Sjonger, Rebecca, *Explore Asia*, Crabtree Publishing, 2007.

About the Author

From vampires to jellybeans, Alicia Klepeis loves to research fun and out-of-the-ordinary topics that bring the world to young readers. Alicia began her career at the National Geographic Society. A former middle school teacher, she is the author of more than seventy children's books including *A Time for Change*, *Trolls*, and *Haunted Cemeteries Around The World*. Alicia has spent time in Singapore, Indonesia, and Japan but hopes to explore more of Asia in the future. She lives with her family in upstate New York.

Meet The Author!
www.meetREMauthors.com

© 2019 Rourke Educational Media

www.rourkeeducationalmedia.com

PHOTO CREDITS: Cover & Title Pg ©By cloki, ©southtownboy, ©By Anna Kucherova, ©dblight, ©kapulya, ©visualspace, Top Bar ©fergregory, Pg 4 ©PeterHermesFurian, Pg 5 ©By dikobraziy, Pg 6 ©kapulya, Pg 7 ©panso, ©Danielrao, Pg 8 ©FilippoBacci, Pg 9 ©By Azhar Hassan, ©Zoran Kolundzija, Pg 10 ©Freder, Pg 11 ©fotoVoyager, Pg 12 ©Andrew_Mayovskyy, Pg 13 ©da-kuk, ©hadynyah, Pg 14 ©FredFroese, Pg 15 ©wiki, Pg 16 ©By Aznan, Pg 17 ©By thebigland, ©Zurijeta, Pg 18 ©ferrantraite, Pg 19 ©pidjoe, Pg 20 ©NicolasMcComber, Pg 21 ©By Tinseltown, Pg 22 ©izamon, Pg 24 ©SJPailkar, Pg 25 ©By Sainam51, Pg 26 ©szefei, Pg 28 ©Leonid Andronov, Pg 29 ©MikeFuchslocher

Edited by: Keli Sipperley
Cover and Interior design by: Rhea Magaro-Wallace

Library of Congress PCN Data

Asia / Alicia Klepeis
(Earth's Continents)
ISBN 978-1-64156-406-9 (hard cover)
ISBN 978-1-64156-532-5 (soft cover)
ISBN 978-1-64156-656-8 (e-Book)
Library of Congress Control Number: 2018930427

Rourke Educational Media
Printed in the United States of America,
North Mankato, Minnesota

5